SO WHAT IS JUSTICE ANYWAY?

CHELSEA LUTHRINGER

the rosen publishing group / rosen central

new york

Published in 2000 by The Rosen Publishing Group, Inc.
29 East 21st Street, New York, NY 10010

First Edition

Luthringer, Chelsea
        So what is justice anyway? / Chelsea Luthringer.
            p.   cm. -- (A student's guide to American civics)
        Includes bibliographical references and index.
        Summary: Discusses the concept of justice, its role in daily life, differing views of justice, how governments achieve justice, and individuals and organizations that have worked for justice.
        ISBN 0-8239-3096-3
        1. Justice Juvenile literature. [1. Justice.] I. Title.
    II. Series.
    JC578.L87 1999
    320'.01'1--dc21   99-31309
                                                                CIP

Manufactured in the United States of America

CONTENTS

INTRODUCTION
OF THE PEOPLE, BY THE PEOPLE, FOR THE PEOPLE

The government of the United States is a democracy. A democracy is a government that is run by the people who live under it. In the United States, we elect representatives who deal with issues that concern us, create laws to protect us, and represent us and our beliefs to the rest of the world.

In a democracy, every citizen is entitled to certain rights and freedoms. In the United States, these rights and freedoms are guaranteed by the Bill of Rights. The Bill of Rights is made up of the first ten amendments to the U.S. Constitution. The First Amendment, for example, guarantees the freedom of speech, freedom of the press, freedom to practice the religion of your choice, and the right to assemble peacefully.

Along with these rights comes the responsibility to uphold the country's laws. You can't expect to be given rights and then be allowed to do whatever you want. Such logic upsets the balance of what it means to live in a free country. We balance our personal freedoms with laws and duties for the common good of all citizens. For example, in the United States we have the right to move from one place to another and live where we please without needing government permission. Yet, before we can purchase a car, we have to pass a driver's license examination and obtain a license for the state in which we live and drive.

The introduction to the Constitution

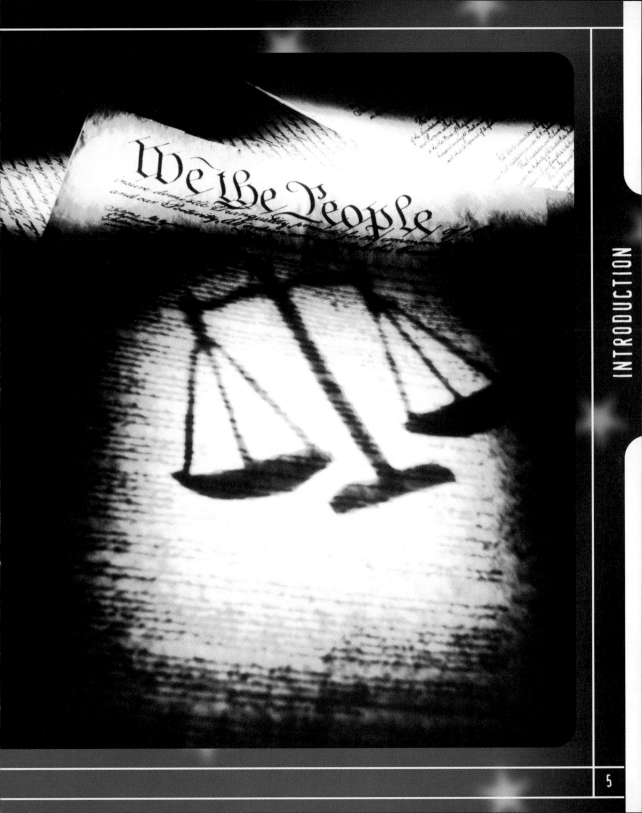

For a democracy to work properly, every citizen must participate in it. There are many ways to participate, and each way is open to everyone.

SOME WAYS TO PARTICIPATE REQUIRE COMMITMENT ON A LARGE SCALE:

✔ Running for political office

✔ Acting as a diplomat (a representative of the United States in another country)

✔ Helping others get elected

✔ Working as a government employee

✔ Voting

OTHER WAYS TO PARTICIPATE ARE THINGS PEOPLE CAN DO EVERY DAY:

✔ Respecting other people

✔ Listening to both sides of an argument before making a decision

✔ Being tolerant of people who are different from you

✔ Treating others fairly

This book discusses the issue of justice. Justice is fairness. The idea of justice is part of every person's life: between individual people, in society, and in government.

so what is justice anyway?

WHAT IS JUSTICE?

The word "just" has several meanings and can be understood many ways. Being just means trying your best to find out the truth or the facts. When you discover something is missing, such as a book or toy, you may wonder if you lost it or if someone borrowed or stole it. You don't want to accuse someone of stealing if you don't know the facts. What if the thing you can't find was simply misplaced by you? Calling someone a thief would be unjust. So you find out the facts before making a decision.

"Just" also means getting what you deserve. Do you receive an allowance from your parents each week for doing chores around the house? If you do, you are being treated justly when the chores have been done and the allowance has been given to you. Likewise, getting what you deserve happens when you have been caught doing something you knew was wrong. The punishment you receive for that mistake is getting what you deserve: punishment for doing wrong.

When you are just, you must also be fair. You are being fair when you share equally in something that you and your friends have bought or have been given. Candy that you divide among you and your friends is a good example. No one person gets more than another.

Mowing the lawn is a chore for many teens that is justly rewarded with an allowance.

CHAPTER ONE

Finally, fairness also means being impartial and reasonable. Impartial means listening to both sides of an argument and not favoring one person over another. Reasonable means reacting in a way that suits the situation.

"I rarely fail any of my students, Thomas," said Ms. Watson. "In this case, however, it's the right thing to do. I saw you and Victor cheating on the exam."

Thomas had always been a top student in Ms. Watson's class. He enjoyed science and usually earned As and Bs on his tests. During the exam today, Ms. Watson had seen Thomas holding up his test in front of him. Then she saw Victor copying Thomas's answers. To be fair to the students in her class, Ms. Watson's policy was to fail students who cheated. It was the only way to make sure that everyone received the grades he or she deserved.

Thomas didn't agree with Ms. Watson's decision. He thought her punishment was unjust. "After I finished the exam," Thomas said, "I read the test over to check my answers. I didn't know Victor was copying my test."

Luckily, Victor agreed that Ms. Watson's punishment was unfair to Thomas. After class, Victor went to Ms. Watson and told her the truth. "Thomas didn't do anything wrong. He didn't know I was copying from his test," Victor insisted.

Ms. Watson was proud that Victor told the truth. She looked over Thomas's exam once more, and gave him an A-. Then she decided to let Victor take the test again. Ms. Watson wanted to reward Victor's honesty by giving him a second chance.

Both Thomas and Ms. Watson wanted to see justice done. Ms. Watson wanted to award grades fairly, according to each student's performance. She believed that a student who didn't study and cheated should not get the same grade as a student who studied and didn't cheat. But Thomas felt that Ms. Watson was punishing him for something he didn't do.

In a just situation, both rewards and punishments are handled fairly. Once Ms. Watson discovered the truth about Victor's cheating, she was able to reward or punish students justly. Thomas received the grade he earned. Victor received a second chance for being honest. Both students felt they had been treated justly.

Finally, Ms. Watson acted impartially by treating both students alike. She also acted reasonably by giving Victor a second chance.

If a test is just, students receive the grades they deserve.

THE FINER POINTS OF JUSTICE

Justice means fairness in both punishment and rewards. One rule of justice demands that the punishment fit the crime. Those who commit no crimes should not be punished. Punishment for those who do commit crimes should be fair, reasonable, and impartial.

Another rule of justice is that rewards should be earned according to what you deserve. For example, a person who does better on a test should get a better grade. It would be unjust, and therefore unfair, for a person's religion, sex, or skin color to affect the grade.

Finally, justice means straightening out disputes fairly. When two people disagree, they should try to settle their disagreement justly. This

Talking out a disagreement often leads to a just agreement.

means settling it based on the facts of the case, and so that each person gets what he or she deserves. It also means settling it fairly, impartially, and reasonably.

SEEING JUSTICE DIFFERENTLY

People often disagree about the best way to receive justice. What one person thinks is fair another person might see as unfair. People also sometimes disagree about the "facts" involved in a particular situation. Ms. Watson thought at first that both Thomas and Victor had cheated on their tests. It was only when she heard more facts that she changed her mind. That is why it is important to try to find out all of the facts before making a decision. Justice depends on finding out the truth.

People can also disagree about what is a fair and just punishment. Some of Ms. Watson's students might have thought it just to fail Victor. After all, he did cheat on the exam. Ms. Watson, however, thought justice would be better served by giving him a make-up test. The important questions of justice include: What are the facts of a given situation? What settlement would be fair?

so what is justice anyway?

JUSTICE IN EVERYDAY LIFE

Justice plays a role in our daily lives on three different levels. The first is the way people deal with one another. The second is the way in which individuals are treated by society. The third is the way in which societies or nations relate to one another. Justice—or injustice—exists on all of these levels.

ONE-TO-ONE
Individuals can treat one another justly or unjustly. Person-to-person justice plays a part in many different relationships. It can involve the relationship between student and teacher, as it did in the case of Thomas and Ms. Watson.

Justice is also present in the relationship between family members. You and your brother fight over who gets to play a video game first. How can this argument be settled justly? Perhaps you can take turns playing, or you can play each other. Either way, you both get what you want. You have settled the argument fairly.

Justice can also be present between a buyer and a seller. Imagine that you traded your copy of the latest CD for your best friend's CD. Later you find out that the CD you traded for was scratched and skipped over

Sharing is a fair way to do a project or play a game.

your favorite song. You would probably feel cheated. How could you correct this injustice? You could ask for your CD back. Or perhaps your friend could give you another CD. Both of these actions would result in greater justice.

SOCIETY TO INDIVIDUALS

Justice is important in the treatment of individuals by the larger society. A society is a group of people who have similar interests and beliefs. A house of worship, a club, and a nation are all examples of societies.

Sometimes societies treat certain individuals unjustly. Some societies punish or torture people for their beliefs or ethnicity or skin color. Since 1998, the ethnic Albanians (people who were born in another country but are Albanian by heritage) in Kosovo, which is a province of the country Serbia, have been killed or forced to leave their country. Ethnic Albanians make up the majority of the population of Kosovo. They would like Kosovo to become a country independent of Serbia. The Serbians, however, believe Kosovo is an important part of their

Kosovo refugees

history and their country. They would rather get rid of the ethnic Albanians than allow Kosovo to become independent. The Serbians have killed hundreds of ethnic Albanians, and forced hundreds of thousands of others to flee their homeland. The Serbians used unnecessary force to stop the ethnic Albanians from creating their own country. This devastated the lives of the two million ethnic Albanians once in Kosovo, their families, and Albanians around the world. By the summer of 1999, this problem was still not solved.

Some societies treat people unjustly because of their gender. Women in England and Canada could not vote in elections until 1918. The United States denied women the vote until 1920. Switzerland did not allow women to vote until 1971. In all four nations, women fought hard to change this injustice.

SOCIETY TO SOCIETY
Societies or nations can also treat each other unjustly. Throughout history, there have been many costly wars because of one society's unjust treatment of another. Nazi Germany, for example, invaded Austria, Czechoslovakia, and Poland in 1938 and 1939. Great Britain and

Nazi forces invading a helpless town in Denmark.

France declared war on Germany within days of the Polish invasion. This war, World War II, soon involved people from almost every part of the world. When the war ended in 1945, more than 35 million people had died in the fight for justice.

Most nations of the world no longer allow individuals to settle disputes through violence. For some nations, however, military force is still used to settle many disputes. Power, rather than truth or justice, decides many international disagreements. The nation that wins a war is not necessarily right. To bring about peace and justice, nations need to work harder to find peaceful means of settling disputes.

American troops land on the beaches of Normandy, France, June 6, 1944.

so what is justice anyway?

THE HISTORY OF JUSTICE

In ancient societies, criminal punishment was the first and most important aspect of justice. These societies had to fight off wild animals and warring neighbors, and struggled against harsh climates. Survival was at stake. The needs of the entire group had to come before the needs of the individual. Providing justice meant punishing crimes committed against the group.

In time the question of survival against harsh natural elements became less threatening. Communities grew larger and more secure. The actions of any one individual seldom threatened the survival of the group. The needs of the group were no longer the only concern of the community. Societies could pay more attention to the positive aspects of justice. This meant rewarding good behavior. And it meant trying to give all individuals what they needed in a fair way.

DIFFERING VIEWS OF JUSTICE

Different societies see justice differently. Justice among the Inuit, a native Arctic people (also called Eskimos), is a good example. Until 1999, when the Inuit were granted the territory of

Inuit hunter

Nunavut, Canada, the Inuit did not believe in the idea of people owning private property. People shared everything to survive. The Inuit did not believe that individuals taking things from the community property was a crime. What a U.S. citizen might call "stealing" was considered survival by the Inuit. However, hurting or killing someone who could hunt and fish was a terrible crime. It could harm the whole community. The Inuit punished people who committed crimes of violence such as these.

There were three kinds of punishment for murder. The first was that the criminal had to provide for the victim's family. The second was death. The third was banishment from the tribe. Banishment meant that the criminal could no longer stay in the community and would have to survive on his or her own. In the harsh climate of the Arctic, being alone nearly always meant a slow death.

Death or banishment of the criminal threatened the group's survival by removing yet another hunter or fisher from the community. However, the Inuit believed that violence was a serious crime. Death or banishment punished the criminal and made others afraid to commit murder.

Not all societies see death as fair punishment, even for murder. Many countries, including Brazil, Portugal, and Switzerland, do not punish any crimes by putting people to death. This is true in many American states, as well. The people of these countries and states do not believe that the fear of death prevents anyone from committing murder. In addition, they see the death penalty as unreasonable punishment.

CHANGING VIEWS OF JUSTICE

Today, justice is also seen as a way to protect the rights of individuals as well as society. Rights are the powers and privileges that all people have simply because they are people. The U.S. Declaration of Independence states that everyone has the right to "life, liberty, and the pursuit of happiness." The justice system in the United States helps make sure people are able to enjoy these rights.

The founding of the United Nations (UN) shows how our views of justice have changed over time. For centuries, war was the main way to settle arguments between nations. War did not, however, determine justice. It did not decide who was fair or right. Military strength, rather than justice, always won.

By 1945, war was no longer believed to be the best way to settle problems between nations. World War II had just ended and millions of people had died. With the threat of nuclear weapons that could destroy the entire planet, war had become much more dangerous.

The UN was founded in 1945 to try to settle disputes more peacefully and fairly and to establish justice among nations without going to war. Today, some disputes are settled by the UN, but many countries, such as Serbia, still choose war to settle differences.

The United Nations building in New York

so what is justice anyway?

Justice and the Legal System

Every society creates rules, or laws, to support and apply its view of justice. Each nation's laws are different because they reflect each society's ideas about justice. While these ideas may change over time, one thing remains the same: People are expected to live by and obey the laws of the country in which they live.

LAWS AND JUSTICE

Laws almost always reflect a society's beliefs. As a society's beliefs change, the laws of the society usually change, too. Laws change to reflect differences in the way a society sees the carrying out of justice. Laws can also change to show the way society thinks about such issues as individual rights, reasonable punishment, and impartiality.

Individual Rights

The first written laws of a society protect society as a whole. They define crimes and set punishments. They also establish a judicial system for the society. The government of a society enforces laws. Its judicial system decides whether laws are applied fairly.

This man is serving time in prison for breaking the law.

More secure societies, however, tend to see justice in the things citizens should do as well as what they should not do. New laws clearly spell out and defend individual rights and freedoms. In this way, laws protect people from power used unfairly against them, especially by governments. Such laws see to it that the individual is treated fairly by society.

Today many nations have passed laws making sure that people's rights are protected. For example, Canada protects individual rights through its Charter of Rights and Freedoms. The United States protects many of these same rights, such as the freedom of speech, writing, and the press, through the Bill of Rights. Such laws say that using these freedoms cannot be called crimes. People cannot be punished for believing or saying or writing what they believe. The right to meet peacefully allows people to protest against unfairness without fear of punishment. These laws try to protect people from the abuse of governmental power.

Reasonable Punishment

The ideas about what punishment fits a crime change from one society to another. They also change over time. The kinds of punishments allowed by a society show how that society understands justice.

Some cultures follow the rules in the Book of Exodus in the Bible: "eye for eye, tooth for tooth . . ." Thieves may have their hands cut off. Those who curse or speak out against God or the government may have their tongues cut out. This kind of "eye for eye" justice still exists in many societies. According to Amnesty International, a human rights organization, punishments such as flogging (beating with a rod or whip), stoning (throwing stones at a person until he or she is dead), and amputations (the cutting off of hands, arms, or legs) are still practiced regularly in

countries such as Saudi Arabia and Yemen.

In a democracy, "eye for eye" punishment is considered revenge rather than punishment. Revenge is not considered a fair or reasonable response to a crime. It is meant to inflict equal—or worse—damage. Revenge is not considered justice.

Many societies have enacted laws that ban the kinds of extreme punishments that they believe to border on revenge. England, Canada, and the United States all forbid the use of "cruel and unusual punishments." These countries believe that such severe punishments would themselves be unjust.

The death penalty is one kind of punishment that has changed, showing a new understanding of justice. Many ancient societies believed that death was an appropriate punishment for murder. It was also considered appropriate for punishing people who were accused of practicing witchcraft or hitting or cursing a parent. Today, the death penalty is regarded by many countries as an unjustly harsh punishment for crimes other than murder. And there are some people who believe that it is an unjust punishment for any crime.

Impartiality

Justice is usually pictured as a blindfolded woman balancing scales. Most cultures, especially democracies, aim toward the idea of the "blindness of justice," or the idea that justice should be impartial. It should be blind to everything but the facts. Justice should be blind in protecting individual rights and delivering punishments. Justice should protect and punish every individual equally. It should not "see" sex, skin color, religion, or wealth. This is the ideal vision of what justice should be in the United States.

In practice, however, justice is not always so blind. Wealth, for example, has a great influence on the process of justice. Crimes committed by the rich are often punished less harshly than those committed by the poor. The wealthy are able to hire more skillful lawyers to defend them. In addition, judges and juries tend to regard wealthy criminals as less of a threat to society and therefore may give them a lesser punishment if they're found guilty. Also, justice is not truly blind to an individual's religion, race, sex, or skin color.

Justice has become more impartial though the efforts of people like Thurgood Marshall. Marshall, a lawyer and former Supreme Court Justice, fought to make justice blind to

Supreme Court Justice Thurgood Marshall

skin color. From 1938 to 1961 he won 29 of the 32 cases he argued before the Supreme Court. Marshall argued that the law must protect the rights of blacks and whites equally. As a result of his cases, blacks won the same rights as whites to vote in primary elections, to sit wherever they want on interstate buses, and to enter law school.

In 1934, Marshall argued his most famous case: *Brown v. Board of Education of Topeka.* After the court's ruling, schools could no longer separate students according to race. It was unjust to let schools deny students an equal education because of their skin color.

No society may ever acheive blind justice, but the United States keeps working toward this goal.

UNJUST LAWS

Justice and the law are not the same thing. Ideally, the law supports justice. However, governments set up laws first to maintain order, and second to promote justice.

Slavery, for example, was part of the way society was organized in the United States until 1865. In that year, following the end of the Civil War, the Thirteenth Amendment to the Constitution ruled that slavery was against the law. Laws before the Civil War preserved slavery. In doing so, the laws of many states allowed white citizens to own slaves. In this way, the United States promoted injustice rather than justice.

There must be laws to protect the common good of any society. But laws must also balance the rights of society and individuals. Laws must also remain fair and impartial. Since not all laws are just, we need to examine our laws with a critical eye. Whenever we discover an unjust law, we have the responsibility to speak out against it.

so what is justice anyway?

Justice Through Government

Most nations try to achieve justice through government. First, governments create general laws that define crimes, protect rights, and set punishments. Second, governments apply these general laws to specific cases.

MAKING LAWS

Many nations, including Canada and the United States, enact new laws according to a written constitution. A constitution states the powers of a government. It is thought of as the highest law of the land. All new laws must follow the laws of a nation's constitution. The constitution guides citizens who make and write the nation's laws.

Many modern constitutions include a bill of rights. This document protects its people from the possible injustice of their government. The English Bill of Rights, passed by Parliament in 1689, limited the power of the king. It also granted certain rights to those accused of crimes, and it guaranteed basic individual freedoms, such as those of speech and writing. Both the United States and Canada based their bills of rights on the English Bill of Rights. These documents have greatly advanced the cause of justice in countries that have them.

The reading of the British Parliament Bill of Rights.

A nation's constitution and bill of rights are guides in the creation of new laws. As our views of justice change over time, our laws also change. Lawmakers must have the means to change general laws so they agree with current ideas and beliefs. There are many examples of this in American history.

Until 1920, women were not allowed to vote in the United States. At that time in American history, the popular belief among those in government was that women were unable to understand the way government works. Therefore, it was believed that women were unable to make good decisions about who should be in government. During the mid- and late-1800s, thousands of women used their First Amendment right to write articles, give speeches, and march peacefully to protest this thinking.

Women suffragists marched to win the right to vote.

PRESIDENT WILSON SAYS: "This is the time to support Woman Suffrage."

PRES... NT "I urge the peo... w York for Woman Suff... k you t...

These women who fought for the right to vote were called suffragists. Suffragists believed that women, as citizens, had the right to have a say in who represented them in the government. Slowly they were able to gain support for this belief. Finally, the Nineteenth Amendment, passed in 1920, gave women the right to vote. This is a good example of how the laws of a society change as its views of what is just change.

SYSTEMS OF JUSTICE

All nations establish judicial systems, or systems of justice, in an attempt to give equal justice to all members of a society. Judicial systems carry out the laws of the land. They apply general laws to specific cases.

The judicial systems of the United States have strong links to the British system of justice. In Great Britain's early history, the king defined what was just. The country's nobles, however, felt that the king did not deliver justice impartially. The nobility were the ruling class of people in English society. To avoid being overthrown, King John signed the Magna Carta (Latin for "great charter") in 1215. The Magna Carta was the first English document

King John signing the Magna Carta

that outlined what people then thought was the "proper" course of justice.

The Magna Carta promised justice to all members of the nobility. It guaranteed accused noblemen the right to a trial by a jury of their peers (their equals). It established trial courts to help deliver justice. Centuries later, England granted these rights to all of its citizens, rather than just its nobles. The United States adopted much of the British judicial system. The workings of trial courts in particular are similar to the British system of justice.

THE COURTS

Most judicial systems employ courts, judges, and juries to deliver justice. The courts in most Western countries do three things: 1) They carry out

A jury box in the courthouse at the Centre Street Supreme Court Building in New York

and enforce the law by trials and sentencing, 2) They attempt to settle disputes fairly and without violence, and 3) They examine laws to make sure they remain just. All three of these may also involve punishing and/or correcting unjust or abusive treatment.

In the United States, both the federal government and individual states operate a number of trial courts—courts in which most trials occur. Federal and local (state) courts try both criminal and civil cases. There are two basic types of courts in the U.S.

Criminal courts

Criminal courts decide cases in which the state or federal government has accused someone of breaking a law. This includes cases of violent crime, such as assault, rape, and murder. Criminal courts also try cases of nonviolent crimes, such as theft, fraud, vandalism, drug selling, spying, and treason (betraying your government).

Civil courts

Civil courts settle disputes between two parties. The law refers to the participants in a civil lawsuit as parties. Parties in a lawsuit may be people, businesses, organizations, or the government. One party, the plaintiff, sues another party, the defendant, for causing damages to its person or property. A broken stair may have caused a neighbor to fall and break a hip. Or perhaps a newspaper printed lies that damaged someone's good name. The party injured by either of these actions can sue to obtain justice. The civil court aims to restore justice peacefully to someone injured by the actions of another.

Sometimes a civil suit involves a criminal action. For instance, someone hit by a drunken driver can sue the driver. The plaintiff may demand money to pay for medical bills or lost wages. In this case, however, the state may still bring criminal charges against the defendant for driving while drunk. The criminal and civil trials would be held separately.

In a criminal or civil trial, lawyers for each side present witnesses, evidence, and arguments in an attempt to prove their case or disprove the other side's case. A judge makes sure that the trial remains fair to both sides. A judge or jury listens to both sides of the disagreement and then decides if any wrong has been done. If the defendant in a criminal trial is found guilty, the judge then decides fair punishment. In a civil suit, if the plaintiff wins, the jury or judge decides what the cost of the damages caused by the defendant should be.

Unfortunately, trial courts do not always deliver justice. When this happens, the case may be appealed, or brought from a lower court to a higher court. Appeals courts serve as watchdogs over all other courts but the Supreme Court. An appeals court reviews trial court rulings to make sure they are fair. Defendants can ask for an appeal if they believe the trial ruling, the sentence, or the award of damages in a civil suit was unfair.

The appeals court judge may agree with the court's decision if he or she believes it has been just. But if he or she decides there is a serious injustice, the appeals court may reverse the court's decision. Or it may order a new trial. Defendants or plaintiffs can appeal the decisions of appeals courts to even higher courts.

The highest court in the United States is the Supreme Court. It has the final word on whether justice has been served. The Supreme Court reviews the rulings in lower court records. It also examines the laws that apply in each case it reviews. The Supreme Court makes sure the laws remain just and agree with the U.S. Constitution. (All courts can strike down laws that violate the Constitution.) The Supreme Court gives the final ruling on the cases it accepts. Defendants or plaintiffs cannot appeal their case any further.

DUE PROCESS

The guarantee of due process is the most important principle of justice of the United States judicial system. Due process, as defined in the Bill of Rights, are the rules that govern our justice system. The rules of due process protect the legal rights of those accused or even suspected of committing a crime. They are used to ensure that everyone gets a fair trial.

One of the most important parts of due process guarantees the accused the right to a jury trial. This right applies to serious criminal cases and to many civil cases. The trial should take place as quickly as possible, because a defendant may be innocent. In addition, the trial should be held in public to help ensure fairness.

A key element of due process is the "presumption of innocence." A judge and jury must always assume the defendant in a criminal trial is innocent until proven guilty. Being charged with a crime is not the same as being guilty of that crime. A defendant's guilt must be proven "beyond a reasonable doubt." The defendant does not have to prove his or her innocence.

No system, including the judicial system, is perfect. It is more effective and just than deciding disputes with fighting or violence. It offers most people some protection from the abuse of power. However, every judicial system has its flaws and mistakes. The courts cannot guarantee justice in every case. Sometimes the police, who are supposed to uphold justice, use undue violence to achieve an end. In February 1999, New York City police shot 22-year-old Amadou Diallo 41 times on the suspicion that he was a rapist they were looking for. He wasn't. Shortly after the shooting, the police officers involved were charged with murder. As of summer 1999, they await trial.

left: the mother of Amadou Diallo
right: the officers indicted for
his murder

FIGHTING FOR JUSTICE

Each of us is responsible for doing what we can to ensure justice. This may mean taking action to defend justice or fight injustice. When a government does not provide justice, the people must attempt to achieve it in some other way.

PROTESTS

The law must protect all people's safety, security, and rights. Laws that fail to provide equal protection to all of a nation's citizens are themselves unjust. Many people refuse to obey laws they consider unjust. Other people practice a form of protest called civil disobedience. This is breaking a law to make a point.

Reverend Jesse Jackson, former New York City Mayor David Dinkins, and 215 other people were arrested on March 26, 1999, for protesting the killing of Amadou Diallo by New York City police officers. They were also protesting what they believe is an increase in police brutality. The protesters blocked the entrance of police headquarters in the hope of being arrested. They believed that being arrested for protesting made their point much stronger. Civil disobedience is an effective method of protest, but should be used only in extreme cases of injustice.

PEOPLE WHO FOUGHT FOR JUSTICE

People who have the courage to stand up for what they believe in can also bring about justice. The champions of justice demand changes to correct injustice. Two such champions of justice were Jane Addams and Martin Luther King, Jr.

Jane Addams, Social Reformer

Jane Addams took up the cause of justice in many ways. In the 1880s, Addams became concerned about the unjust treatment of poor people. The poor were denied proper housing and a good education. Addams felt it was unjust for the poor to have so little when the rich had so much. She became convinced that living among the poor was the only way to ensure that they received justice.

In 1889, Addams opened Hull House in a very poor neighborhood in Chicago. Lawyers, artists, educators, and social workers who lived in Hull House took part in hands-on social reform. Social reformers work to change society to make it more just. They supplied the community

Jane Addams holds a little girl at Hull House.

with day care, gymnasiums, education, and schooling in art and music.

Addams soon realized that providing services was not enough to deliver justice to the poor. Working conditions for poor people were sometimes inhuman. Addams fought for labor laws that would eliminate the abuse of workers by factories and other employers. She demanded child labor laws to protect children from the mistreatment of employers.

Addams also believed that the courts treated children unjustly. She did not think it was fair to treat children who committed crimes as adults. Her crusade against this injustice led to the formation of the nation's first juvenile court in 1899. Addams was awarded the 1931 Nobel Peace Prize for her many efforts to advance the cause of justice.

Dr. Martin Luther King, Jr., Civil Rights Activist

Dr. Martin Luther King, Jr. was a civil rights leader who fought injustice against black Americans in the 1950s and 1960s. He spoke to thousands of people who supported his cause, led marches around the country, and wrote letters and articles asking people to peacefully protest the unfair treatment of black people. One such protest in Birmingham, Alabama, became violent. Police blasted protesters with water

Martin Luther King, Jr.

from fire hoses, used attack dogs, and battered them with nightsticks. Yet thousands of people risked injury, arrest, and death to protest for equal human and political rights.

King and hundreds of others were jailed for their part in the protest. Yet King vowed to continue the struggle despite the unjust violence. He pledged his commitment to justice in his famous "Letter from Birmingham Jail." He smuggled the letter out of jail on scraps of paper, newsprint, and toilet paper. "Injustice anywhere is a threat to justice everywhere," he wrote. King was awarded the Nobel Peace Prize in 1964 for his work. In 1968, he was killed by someone who was afraid of his ideas.

ORGANIZATIONS THAT FIGHT FOR JUSTICE

Organizations can also fight against injustice. The United Nations attempts to promote peaceful and fair interaction among the countries of the world. The UN operates the International Court of Justice, also known as the World Court. This court is intended to settle serious disputes arising between nations in a fair, reasonable, and impartial manner. In this way, nations have a means of obtaining justice without going to war. Membership in the UN has tripled since it was founded in 1945. Today more than 185 countries belong to the United Nations.

Another organization that fights injustice is Amnesty International (AI). Founded in London in 1961, AI fights against government abuse of

AMNESTY INTERNATIONAL

individual rights. AI publicizes violations of human rights and freedoms in countries all over the world. AI is especially concerned about governments that unjustly imprison, torture, and kill people. Members of AI write letters of protest to governments that commit these injustices. Today, Amnesty International, which won the 1977 Nobel Peace Prize, has over one million members in more than 100 countries.

The champions of justice are everywhere and include young people, journalists, artists, mothers, students, lawyers, and former convicts. You, too, can stand up for justice.

Look around your own neighborhood. Do you notice any injustice there? Perhaps the local deli refuses to let students enter the store without supervision. Maybe a local club refuses to admit certain people as members because of the color of their skin. Or perhaps another student is taking credit for something you know he or she did not do. Whenever you notice injustices like these, fight them. Stand up for what you know is right.

GLOSSARY

amendment A change to something.

bill of rights A document that lists and protects the individual rights of people.

civil court A state or federal court in which disputes between two parties are resolved.

constitution A document stating a government's powers.

criminal court A state or federal court that determines whether an accused person has committed a crime.

defendant A party that is being sued by another party in a civil court, or a person who is charged with a crime in a criminal court.

democracy A government that is run by the people who live under it.

dispute A situation in which two people or parties do not agree.

due process The rules that govern a justice system; the rules that protect the legal rights of those accused or suspected of committing a crime.

impartial Showing no more favor to one side than to the other.

judicial system The body of government that determines whether laws are applied fairly to people.

jury A group of citizens selected to hear evidence in a case brought before a court of law.

party A person, business, organization, or government involved in a civil court case.

plaintiff A party that sues another party in a civil court.

protest A statement or act in which a person or group objects strongly to something.

reasonable Sensible.

revenge An act meant to inflict pain or damage on someone.

revolt The act of rebelling.

right Something to which a person is entitled.

society A group of people who have similar interests and beliefs.

suffragist A person who fights for the right to vote.

trial The examining and deciding of a case in court.

FOR FURTHER READING

Atgwa, Paul. *Stand Up for Your Rights*. Chicago: World Book, Inc., 1998.

Barker, Dan. *Maybe Right, Maybe Wrong: A Guide for Young Thinkers.* Amherst, NY: Prometheus Books, 1992.

———. *Maybe Yes, Maybe No: A Guide for Young Skeptics.* Amherst, NY: Prometheus Books, 1990.

Bradley, Catherine. *Freedom of Movement*. Danbury, CT: Franklin Watts, Inc., 1998.

Dunn, Lynne. *The Department of Justice*. New York: Chelsea House Publications, 1989.

Gordon, Vivian V. and Lois Smith-Owens. *Prisons and the Criminal Justice System.* New York: Walker and Company, 1992.

Greebly, Keith Elliot. *Adolescent Rights: Are Young People Under the Law?* New York: Twenty-first Century Books, 1995.

Hirst, Mike. *Freedom of Belief*. Danbury, CT: Franklin Watts, Inc., 1998.

Jacobs, William Jay. *Great Lives: Human Rights*. Old Tappan, NJ: Atheneum, 1990.

O'Connor, Maureen. *Equal Rights.* Danbury, CT: Franklin Watts, Inc., 1998.

RESOURCES

AMERICAN CIVIL LIBERTIES UNION (ACLU)
125 Broad Street, 18th Floor
New York, NY 10004-2400
(212) 549-2585
Web site: http://www.aclu.org/

COALITION FOR FEDERAL SENTENCING REFORM
3125 Mt. Vernon Avenue
Alexandria, VA 22305
(703) 684-0373
Web site: http://www.sentencing.org/

Web Sites
UNITED NATIONS
http://www.un.org/

AMNESTY INTERNATIONAL
http://www.amnesty.org/

JUSTICE DEPARTMENT INFORMATION CENTER
http://ncjrs.aspensys.com/

INDEX

ABOUT THE AUTHOR

Chelsea Luthringer is a freelance writer in New York. She is the author of two Rosen Central books for young adults.

PHOTO CREDITS

Design and Layout

Kim M. Sonsky

Consulting Editors

Mark Beyer and Jennifer Ceaser